It Didn't Break Me

MY PERSONAL STRUGGLE WITH
DEPRESSION AND HOW ONE WORD
FROM GOD CHANGED MY LIFE

Jennifer M. Jackson

REJOICE
Essential Publishing

Copyright © 2022 by Jennifer M. Jackson

Jennifer M. Jackson/Rejoice Essential Publishing
PO BOX 512
Effingham, SC 29541

www.republishing.org

Unless otherwise indicated, scripture is taken from the King James Version.

It Didn't Break Me/Jennifer M. Jackson

ISBN-13: 978-1-956775-33-4

LCCN: 2022913911

Endorsement

"It Didn't Break Me" is truly an empowering and inspirational story that will touch your heart and reassure you of God's healing power. Through Jennifer Jackson's powerful testimony, God's love, purpose, and healing power shine through each chapter.

I believe that when we are obedient to God in telling our stories, lives are impacted and transformed, hope is imparted, and God is glorified.

It is truly a courageous story filled with hope. The Bible reminds us that there is hope to be found even in the darkest of days of our lives. That HOPE that lives on the inside of us is Christ. He is a healer.

This book will touch the hearts of so many who have traveled the same path of brokenness and who need healing.

— **Carol Davis**
Founder, Writing To Inspire

Dedication

*T*HIS BOOK IS DEDICATED to God, Jesus, and The Holy Spirit for not allowing me to fall and putting excellent Leaders (Spiritual and Military) and Soldiers in my life and path.

To the memory of Mr. Isiah and Maudie Mae Jackson, who opened not only their home to me but gave me a sure foundation. Keeping me in church and making sure Jesus was foremost in my life.

To the memory of Pastor Betty, who at one Bible study spoke a word in my life that she knew I wasn't trying to receive. I thank God for obedience and listening to the voice of the Lord. God used her to push me out of a dark place so that God could begin the work He purposed to do in my life.

To the memory of Ms. Annice H. Jones, while vacationing in Hawaii, visiting her daughter and family (Rodney and Veronica "Chrissy" Brown) became an intracule part of keeping me grounded and getting back into church after that being the last place, I wanted to be in. Her love, support, and firmness always reminded me that sometimes God must shift us in an uncomfortable position to get us to our purpose.

Through a move of God, Rodney and Veronica "Chrissy" Brown became a part of my life when I was looking for a babysitter while stationed in Hawaii. When I looked back on the way God opened a spot for Johnathan to be in their care, all I can say is BUT GOD. To this day, we are forever connected.

My kindergarten teacher, Mrs. Mary Sue Boles, was a God-sent in my life. A driving force that pushed me into getting my degree in education.

I call the three musketeers Cassandra Polanco, Davilyn Godinet, and Wynyeh Williams. We were a shop of all females, and it was a blast. I don't see three ladies as my former Soldiers, but as my three little sisters. They motivated me as their supervisor. They all had their personalities, but we always worked together. I could leave the shop in their hands, not fearing that all craziness would break loose. When people ask me why I stayed in the military past 20 years, I think of these three, my little sisters.

Apostle Jesse and Pastor Shawn Camarillo came into my life while I was stationed in Germany back in 2006. Their presence in my life has truly been a gift from God! Their words of firmness, correction, and love have always kept me grounded. I can always expect them to keep it real with me.

Apostle Warren and Pastor Linda Thames, there is so much I can say about them, and it would take more than this to describe their love for me. God brought them into my life in 2009 when I was stationed in Fort Hood! All I can say is Thank You Lord. They are not only my leaders, but I consider them as parents. I can always trust them to be transparent and real with me. Even in the wisdom, guidance, firmness, and correction, I always know it comes from a place of love. They continue to push me to go forward in who God says I am and called to be.

My son Johnathan always gave me a reason to keep pushing and moving forward.

We might not understand why we go through things in life, but God always has a way of showing us that our lives are a testament to His goodness and faithfulness.

Table of Contents

Foreword

INISTER JENNIFER JACK-
SON IS an awesome Woman
of God. My family and I have
known Miss Jackson for over twenty years. She
is a Mother, Teacher, Praise Dancer, Evangelist and Prayer Warrior who genuinely loves to
serve God's people.

Those who are blessed to have crossed paths
with her can attest that she is an amazing individual who teaches others to live a godly life. I
believe the book will inspire, bring healing, and
add invaluable insight to those who are struggling with spiritual attacks that come against the
mind. Jennifer is truly inspirational and a wonderful gift from God, given to help His people.

—Pastor Shawn Camarillo

Redeemed Faith Ministries

Preface

BEFORE THE DOOR OPENS

BEFORE I CAN FULLY go into these chapters, let alone this book, I must share with you my transparent moment. Today is the 28th day of April 2019, and I am up early doing my usual morning workout. I just completed my run and finished it off with a nice cool-down walk, and I started balling into tears. I can feel the Spirit of the Lord pressing upon me that there is no shame in sharing what He has told me to release. Fear totally had me bound, and I was reluctant to even write this book. A part of me was fearful that the doors I had closed from my past would open back up and try to take hold of me and pull me back to a place I honestly had to fight my way through spiritually. I could hear the voice of the Lord telling me, "I have you and there is no need for fear. This book isn't about you, but it's about the lives I want to change through you, telling your testimony about me." So, needless to say, I had to get out of my feelings and do what the Lord has told me to do...Now on to my story!

Introduction

HAVE YOU EVER WONDERED if people could see what was truly going on inside of you by looking at the outside? Every day you wake up feeling like you're going around the same merry-go-round, only hoping that someone would press the stop button. Well, there are many people on this merry-go-ground of life only wanting it to stop so they can just scream, "Lord, where are you?" It seems like your life is filled with so many ups and downs, but you are still here living, or should I say "functioning."

This is exactly how I felt at times growing up, and even during my adult life, I felt this way while I had a smile on my face. I had gotten to the point where all I was doing was functioning until it became a part of me just "living." You could even say I had "a one day at a time" mentality. It's easy to put a smile on your face when you know you truly need to reach out and ask for help. What is that help going to look like? Are they going to judge me because I am the "strong" one, always ready to help others, but fearful of what people would think about me?

Growing up, I had plenty of ups and downs, and I would question God, asking Him, "Did you bring me into the world for this?" Why does it seem like nothing in my life is going right? Feeling like you don't fit in is very difficult, but for a child, it can be hurtful and hugely impactful on your life. With all these feelings I had inside of me, one area in my life that was life-changing was being placed in foster care. You may be thinking, "wow," and yes, you are right to say, "Wow." My first introduction to Christ was while I was in foster care. I remember getting my first Bible, and I was excited because it had my name on it. Honestly, my first Bible was one of the greatest gifts I have ever received.

As you read that sentence, reflect on the one thing you have received that still has a lasting impact on your life even until this day. Many of us have been through things in life that should have made us want to give up. I mean, completely throw in the towel and walk away from everything, even down to the thought of locking yourself away from the world. For some of you, you may have also contemplated suicidal feelings, as if the world would be better without you in it. However, you are still alive to say, "I made it. I don't know how, but I am here."

Life is full of ups and downs. Deuteronomy 31:6 (KJV) says, "Be strong and of a good courage, fear not, nor be afraid of them: for the Lord thy God, he it is that doth go with thee; he will not fail thee, nor forsake thee." One thing you can hold as real is the fact that God is always present even when we don't think or feel He is there. That's one place the enemy truly loves to torment your mind is with thoughts that God is mad at you, or He doesn't love you because of your actions. This fact is far from true. When you find yourself in this place, this is genuinely when you must press in and seek Him.

You may be thinking, "Well, how do you find that place when everything around you seems like it's breaking, and it's starting in your mind?" You're at the point when you feel like you are truly going crazy and about to snap. It was in this place, I genuinely had to ask for God's help! I was at a place in my life where I thought my life was meant for all hurt and nothing good.

During this time in my life, I truly wanted to throw my hands up and throw in the towel. I wanted my life to be over, so no one would have to deal with me at all. I was dealing with people who I knew I didn't need to be involved with, but my self-esteem was so low I was grateful for the attention. I felt as though God could have given my son a better mom because I didn't feel like I was good enough. One day I had a "come to Jesus moment," and it was as if the light bulb came on so bright. I couldn't miss Him.

One thing I will tell you about God is that when there is purpose in your life, He won't give up on you. It was as if God was strategically bringing key people into my life at the right time when I needed it the most. The enemy only comes to kill, steal and destroy, but the Lord comes to give your life and life more abundantly (John 10:10). The only way the enemy can have power over you is if you willfully provide that power to him.

You may be in a place in your life right now and don't know how you have made it this far. It may seem like one moment you're up, and then you're down. Storms appear as though they follow you everywhere you turn. I tell you that if you are reading this book, then you are at that place to where what could have broken you only became the driving force of your determination and by the power of the Holy Spirit.

This is your day for a breakthrough. Realize that God has been on your side, and you have a God-given purpose to live and be free to walk in the life God purposed for you. So, no more looking back. This is a season of moving forward in the things of God. Life didn't break you, but it opened the door for God's glory to reign forth in your life.

CHAPTER 1

You Don't Know My Story

THE LORD HAD GIVEN me the topic of this book back in 2017 while on deployment in Afghanistan. I had finished up my morning workout, and the Holy Spirit said, "It didn't break me." Of course, me being the over-thinker that I am at times, I was trying to figure out what He was honestly saying. Yes, as time went by, I thought about what I heard and put it on the shelf. In December 2018, God opened a tremendous door of opportunity to write. I was watching a periscope of Prophetess Kimberly Moses, and she was speaking about her latest book, "It Cost Me Everything." She was opening the opportunity up for coauthors to write a chapter in the book. I could hear the

Lord so clearly telling me, "This is for you!" Of course, me being me, I was going back and forth with, "Should I or shouldn't I?" Well, I got that push, "Yes, you are." After going through the list of topics available to write about, and most of them, I could relate to because I had allowed myself to get caught up in them. However, the one topic that the Lord shined a bright light on was depression.

At first, I was scared and ashamed because, for the people who know me, they would genuinely be shocked that I had battled depression and even contemplated suicide at one point in my life. However, The Lord said, "NO! This is your topic, and you are going to write about it. I have you. This is about helping other people who are struggling and need to know that there is more on the other side of the mountain."

During the earlier part of 2018, there was a lot of news coverage of leaders in prominent positions in churches, the fashion industry, culinary world, and more who had taken their life only to find out that they were battling with depression. For some in the world, it was a shock because by looking at their lives, you wouldn't imagine that they also had struggles. Yes, they were making money from the fashion line, the five-star restaurants, and even bringing the Word of God, telling their members about the goodness of God, yet they were battling their own personal demon.

Depression doesn't care about how much money you make, how good you can take a design and bring it to life, how good you can take a recipe, or even a song and have it come forth like magic. Depression doesn't care about how eloquently you can deliver the Word of God with such passion across the pulpit or television, having people coming to the altar to give their lives to Christ, all the while, you need help. You need someone to see the true you. Depression is a Spirit and mood disorder that robs you of your life, peace and keeps you from those who genuinely love you. It also keeps you from seeing your true God-given purpose and the wonderful person you are to become.

In biblical times there were great and mighty men and women of God who were significantly used by Him, and they dealt with depression. We need to lose the mindset and this way of thinking that only a "certain" type of person deals with depression. Even the most "saved" person in the world can be hit with the spirit of depression. The enemy will play with your mind to the point that you will believe what he is saying and showing you. Just as Romans 2:11 (KJV) says, "For there is no respecter of persons with God." There is also no respecter of persons when it comes to depression. There is one key difference. God sent Jesus into the world so that we could have life and have it more abundantly (John 10:10). The enemy's key goal is to come and steal the life God has promised. He wants to kill and destroy us by any means necessary. We must hold on to the hand of God and know that He is for us and not against us.

Growing up as a child, I would have never thought I was suffering from what I know now as depression. I honestly just thought I was a sad child with anger issues, who talked a lot and was always getting sent home from school because of my behavior in the classroom. Elementary school was a struggle for me because I was always getting into trouble, and it seemed like it was around second grade or so. Acting out in the way I did was almost like a cover for how I was feeling, and I knew I would face the consequences when I got home. Now that I look back on my actions, I can see that I was battling within myself and the pain that came from holding secrets in. I was also dealing with rejection and feeling like I just didn't fit in anywhere. I mean, I had friends at school who I played with, but I can see now how I was desperate for attention. If you knew me growing up in school, my name at some point ended up on the blackboard because of my behavior in the classroom and entirely not following or even attempting to follow the instructions given in the school. It was to the point the principal would have to bring me home at times. Once I got to middle school, "junior high" is when things started to change for me. I will talk about that in a later chapter.

Throughout life, we encounter so many different people in various stages and times. People looking at you, seemingly thinking that you have it all together, not even knowing that there is a part of you that is screaming out for help, wondering, can you truly see the pain in my eyes? Or are they so used to seeing that strong-willed person who seems ready to take on any challenge or obstacle that comes your way? All the while, you are thinking within yourself, "I truly just want to give up and throw in the towel." I have had all I can take at this point in my life. We all come from many different backgrounds, cultures, and ethnicities, etc. All with a different perspective, from growing up hearing, "What happens in this house, stays in this house. We ain't keeping up with the Jones'." Most of us have heard that respective saying, and we knew loud and clear what the consequences were if what happened at home was out in public. Or maybe you have never heard that saying and you knew within yourself some things are just better kept quiet.

Growing up, I learned to keep things to myself because there was that part of me that felt like I wouldn't be believed at all. I mean, come on. I was getting in trouble in school, so why should anyone believe me? I was making things up to get attention when all the while, I had a secret that was killing me to the point that I wanted to be by myself. In a nutshell, that was me growing up as a child, even into my adult life. I had so many secrets locked up on the inside of me that it was so unbearable that at times I convinced myself that I brought it all on myself. I can remember asking God, "Why did you create me the way you did?" I was angry at God because I felt as if my body was shaped differently, or if I physically looked different, I wouldn't get any attention. I had to learn that no matter what I looked like, it wouldn't stop that person from viewing and seeing me any differently. Let's face it. In today's society, people are very visual and often moved by what they see. I can remember as a child growing up in foster care, feeling like I was incredibly different and that I didn't fit in.

I ended up in foster care as a toddler with my baby brother because my mom couldn't take care of us at the time. Although she did her best, it got to the point where the state realized we needed to be in a stable home. One thing I will share about foster care is that I know each state is different in their procedures and placement. There are times when siblings are placed in separate foster homes for various reasons, and this was almost the case with me and my younger brother on my mom's side. My younger brother was going to the Jackson's, and I was supposed to be going to the William's. Now the "God move" in this for me is that they were out of town, and they still needed a home to place me in. With the William's being out of town, the social worker asked the Jackson's about taking me into their home as well, and it was all the Lord wrote. I say it was a God move because He already knew I was going into their home. It was the place I would find Him as a child growing up and not forgetting about Him in my adult life.

Being in the Jackson's home was indeed a God move as stated previously! You may be thinking, "How can that be a God move?" I say it's a God move because He will put you in the place He wants you to grow and knows the environment where that will happen. I received my first Bible with my name on it, engraved in gold. I was so excited when I received my Bible. It truly meant the world to me because me and papa would read together, and he would help me with scriptures. The wisdom that he gave showed me how important it is to have a relationship with the Lord.

I can remember learning "Now I Lay Me Down To Sleep" as well as The Lord's Prayer. God has forever been present, and a part of my life. There are things in our lives that can shake us to the point where we start questioning God. I didn't have all the "cool" clothes like others around me, and I will admit that there was a part of me that was jealous of those kids because they had things I wanted. Let's be honest. It was things I thought I should have, but it doesn't always work that way in life. You get what God gives you and live. During my time in foster care before I got adopted, I would visit my biological mother to see if she could keep me with her permanently. The Jacksons already had adopted my younger brother, who was already in foster care with me. My mom was just in a place in her life where she couldn't keep both of her children, and I indeed hold no hatred or malice towards her. I know she did the best she could. Often you have stories of children who knew their biological parents and ended up hating them.

One of the most impactful moments in my life, while I was in foster care, was when my biological father would come and visit, and there was a part of me that thought I would live with him one day, and of course, that never happened. I can remember him coming to visit. He had a khaki shirt and pants on, sitting in my papa's chair, and the last thing I remembered was getting a white cape and $40. That was the turning point about how I saw myself because I never heard from him after that. This is the place where I can reflect and say that the seed of rejection had taken root in my life, and it was in a bad way.

CHAPTER 2

The Visit That Changed My Life

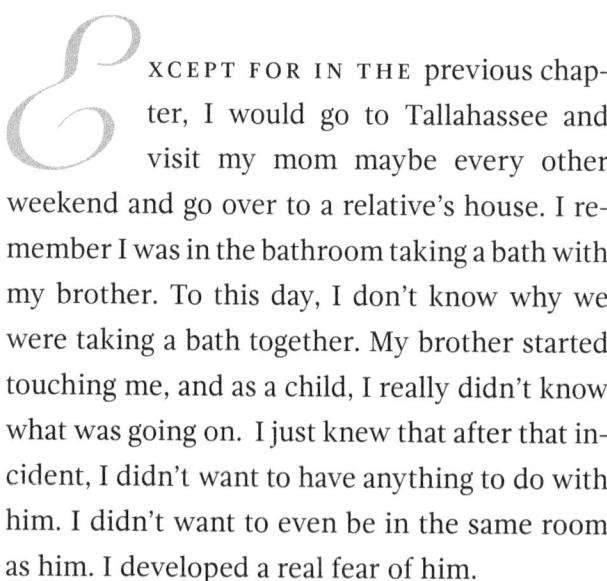

EXCEPT FOR IN THE previous chapter, I would go to Tallahassee and visit my mom maybe every other weekend and go over to a relative's house. I remember I was in the bathroom taking a bath with my brother. To this day, I don't know why we were taking a bath together. My brother started touching me, and as a child, I really didn't know what was going on. I just knew that after that incident, I didn't want to have anything to do with him. I didn't want to even be in the same room as him. I developed a real fear of him.

During that visit, I had the opportunity to say something, but I kept it to myself. I remember being with my mom at one of my friend's house, and she was sitting next to him on the couch. I was on the other end, holding onto the arm of the chair with my legs crossed so no one could come near me. I remember her asking me what was going on and why I didn't want to sit next to her. I remember holding on to the chair and looked at her and said, "I am fine." I knew I wasn't okay. I just wanted to go back to Panama City and never return to Tallahassee. Not only was that the place I was molested, but it was the place where my rejection was planted. When I got back home, I never said anything. I locked that weekend up inside of me. During the counseling session I was attending, I never opened up about that weekend. I just kept it all locked up inside and hated myself. When something is so painful, it's easy for the person to question just exactly what they did wrong.

My behavior began to change at that point. I don't know if it was because I was protecting myself by projecting my hurt on other people. I only knew that I was hurting inside. I was already battling with my weight, and food had become a source of comfort for me growing up. It was a great way to hide the pain I was truly feeling. I had so much hatred for myself boiling on the inside of me. I was given the nickname "truck" growing up, and it truly made me self-conscious of my weight and how I truly felt about myself. I look back at pictures with the Kool-Aid smile, but there was always that part of me that hated myself.

The insecure little girl questioned God as to why I had to be violated? What did I do to make my brother, my blood brother, want to violate me? This act opened the door to where I was experiencing sleep paralysis, and I can remember vividly, trying to break free. At that point in my life as a little girl, I didn't know and truly understand that calling on the name of Jesus had the power to set me free. I became utterly fearful of sleeping in my bed because I was terrified of being held down in my own bed, unable to move and speak.

At times, I would sneak into my papa and grandma's room, with my blanket and sleep on the floor next to them because that was the only place I truly felt safe at nighttime. Of course none of this helped with the fact that I would watch scary movies. I remember telling papa I was scared to sleep in my room at night, but I wasn't telling him that I was experiencing sleep paralysis. He would tell me to say my prayers, as well as sleeping with the Bible under my pillow, opened to Psalms 23. If you could see those pages today, you can see where they are worn down, and the ink looks blurred because of it being under my pillow at night so I could sleep.

My fear of sleeping had gotten to the point where I had to sleep with a night light on to be able to sleep and stay in my room. I felt like the devil was after me, and I didn't know what to do. I would have dreams about hell and I was indeed scared of dying because, honestly, I had it made it up in my mind that I was going to hell. On top of all this, I was still functioning in church as a member in the choir and youth usher board. I was still dealing with the spirit of fear and was fearful of sleeping.

CHAPTER 3

I Got A New Name

I DON'T KNOW WHAT THE exact day was, and the month may have been August or September. I just know my name went from Washington to Jackson. I remember this day so clearly down to what I was wearing and even my hairstyle. I had on some lavender shaded shorts with white stripes on them and a white shirt with pastel color patches, and my hair was in two braids. After the paperwork was signed by the judge, I shook his hand, and he called me Jennifer Michelle Jackson. That was one of the happiest days of my life. I went to school the following day and it took some time getting used to my new last name being Jackson.

Now life had to get back to "normal," but my normal was being fearful of sleeping and letting anyone know what was going on inside of me. My behavior was still a problem. Being in Mrs. Parker's third-grade class, there seemed like there wasn't a time I didn't get in trouble for my behavior. Often, my behavior led to me receiving a paddling and reflecting on it. Now I deserved everyone I received. Of course, when I got home, I received another punishment and they were all well deserved.

With the behavior and discipline issues, I ended up going to counseling because of that as well. Did counseling help? Yes and no! The advice helped me to point out how I was feeling and why I was having issues, but it didn't help me with the fact I was still keeping the secret of being molested. It was just a part of me that I didn't want to share because of shame, and I thought who would believe me if I told them. Too often, we hold on to things for far too long and it becomes a place of bondage and despair. Then there is that part of you that wants to protect those around you from being impacted negatively. After being adopted, that was a part of my life that I didn't want to go back to anymore.

Ultimately, I was impacted because honestly, I hated going to Tallahassee. Tallahassee was a place of hurt and mistrust. Although I had grown up and didn't remember the face of all my relatives or the ones I interacted with when I would go visit. I prayed not to hear the Washington name. I know it sounds so heartless, but that was in my heart growing up. If I didn't have to hear or say the name, I was safe in my mind and heart. Now, if papa and grandma heard me saying anything negative, I would get in a whole lot of trouble because they didn't play that at all.

Growing in Christ and understanding forgiveness and how to let God heal me, I can come in and go to Tallahassee. Plus, I have other family members there on my biological father's side who I had bonded with, my baby brother on my dad's side of the family and his family. I know if I had held onto unforgiveness, I wouldn't have the relationship with them that I have now, and it's one of the best ones I could ever ask for.

CHAPTER 4

School Days

EVERYONE HAS THEIR TAKE on how they view school; either you love it or like it. School for me had both its ups and downs. Kindergarten, by far, was the best time for me. That's when I met the one teacher who impacted my life and still does until this day: Mrs. Mary Sue Boles (aka Mrs. Gast). Mrs. Boles had a presence about her that radiated when she was in the classroom and made learning fun. Being in foster care at the time, she made being different from the other kids, okay. What I mean about being different is not living with my biological parents.

I didn't have all the fancy things that some of the other students had, but I just wanted to fit in class. During the Christmas holidays, some of the kids in foster care would go on a trip to one of the local shopping centers, Gaylord's or Sears to use a voucher to purchase clothes. I didn't feel ashamed about being one of the kids who went on the trip. Again, Mrs. Boles just made being in class and around the other students good. I can honestly appreciate the fact that she would let papa and grandma know when I was acting up and talking a lot in class. Most of all, for the truth, when she realized I wasn't ready to move on to the first grade. With me going back and forth to Tallahassee, a lot was going on, and being prepared for the next grade is extremely important for any child in school.

Amazingly enough back in June of 2016, I had come home to attend grandma's funeral. While in Walmart waiting in line, I see Mrs. Boles, and she sees me, and the tears start falling. Even during grandma's passing, she was able to put a smile on her face. I reconnected to the one person who impacted my life in such a powerful way, even to this day. She is also one of the reasons I pursued my degree in Early Childhood Education. She was beaming with joy when I told her about getting my degree in education. One thing

I've learned and truly understand is that even people outside of our families can have such a profound effect on a person's life.

Now that kindergarten is over, it's when you start going up in age and grades. We truly change. Going through elementary up to high school, you try and find your place amongst your peers. I know I was no different from any other student trying to make it day-by-day going through school, trying to focus on grades, and make it to the next grade level. Now that I look back on my middle school years, I wasn't meant to try and fit in with people, but for me growing up, it almost seemed like a must. I had classmates in school who I considered to be genuinely close friends, and they never gave me a reason to doubt their sincerity towards me.

All that changed during my eighth-grade school year. This was the year that I purposed to change the way how people saw me and viewed me as a person. My behavior and actions were nothing to brag about because from sixth to seventh grade, I seemed to stay in trouble for my mouth and actions. During those years, I spent a lot of time getting suspended and spending time in detention. I was either being belligerent, disrespectful, or talking too much. My behavior was so bad that I caught myself trying to fight someone in the morning before school started thinking it wouldn't get to the disciplinary principal. Now that was the dumbest notion I could ever imagine. Of course, it got to the principal, and I was on my way home, suspended from school. Honestly, it was nothing to brag about, but even as a child, I had an understanding that it was time to make a change for the better.

Eighth grade was the true changing point in my life. I was around thirteen at the time, getting ready to head to high school the following year. I reached the breaking point that I didn't want to be labeled as a "bad student." The highlight and lowlight of my eighth-grade year were receiving the "The Most Improved Eight Grade Student" award. I wasn't expecting that award, but I was extremely excited because I didn't know my teachers and school faculty were watching me and saw a real change in not only my behavior but in my grades as well. All of that came tumbling down with one flip in a yearbook. One of my classmates asked me to sign their yearbook. I can remember so vividly, even until this day, flipping to the page with my picture, seeing the words "FAT PIG" in quotations. I flipped through the pages so quickly because I didn't want them to know what I saw. The part that really hurt was I knew the handwriting of the person who wrote on my picture.

It was tough to come back from that one person seeing me in that manner. I honestly thought this person and me were friends. I mean, we practically grew up together throughout elementary school. Throughout school, both primary and middle, I struggled with my weight. I went home crying after, and that just made me not like myself even more because of what someone who I thought of as a friend, truly felt about me. In my mind, I was asking myself, "Is this how people truly felt and thought of me as well?" I mean, growing up, I was given the nickname "truck." As I reflect on even that name, it was nothing but the grace of God that I was able to put away that name. Did it come up with my struggles? Yes, it did, but I was able to move forward. In that moving forward, I became more depressed, and I gained even more weight during that summer before entering high school.

Here starts the high school years. I enjoyed my freshman year of high school, especially my government class. It was the highlight of my school year. Minus the fact, I had perfect attendance, as well as the right grades needed to not have to take any final exams. The teacher I had for my government class was a Republican, and although I wasn't at the legal age to vote, you knew my standpoint was a Democrat. The best part of his class is when he signed my yearbook, and he so eloquently wrote, "Maybe one day, you will see the light and vote Republican." Well, all I could do was laugh because that wasn't going to happen. At the end of the school year, I had an "A" in his class. I owe part of that A to papa, who kept me involved in politics, always watching the news, CNN. And I can't forget about C-SPAN. Now, maybe for some people, they would've felt some type of way, but I knew he wasn't trying to be malicious. Through the class, we had back and forth conversations on our views, even though they didn't often line up together.

I go from my teacher signing my yearbook laughing, and then to a classmate's yearbook with yet another eighth-grade moment with someone yet again writing on my picture. This time the individual called me a "Fat B@#&$." Yes, I was completely done after that. I mean just done. At that point, I didn't know what to think. What did I do to make people feel this way about me? I hit rock bottom at that point. I already knew how I looked in my yearbook picture. I mean, I bought a yearbook myself and saw the weight in my face. That comment on my photo was the cherry on top of the icing on the cake. One evening following that, I was sitting outside on the patio, and it's still so vivid to me today. I was at the point of suicide. No one knew just how deep down inside I truly hated myself, and I didn't want to live anymore. I broke down and told God, "It's okay if you don't wake me up." I just wanted to die. I felt that God made a big mistake by bringing me into the world.

At this point, rejection had set in and attached itself to my depression state, and I wanted my life to end. I was at the point I was telling the

Lord how wrong He was for bringing me into this world. I told Him, "My mom couldn't keep me and my dad didn't want me. Why am I even here? You let me be born into all of this? Lord, please, it's okay if you don't wake me up. The world will be completely okay if you take my life." I was done with trying to please people. Of course, He didn't listen to me because I am still here. I'm still breathing. I don't know what happened from my freshman to sophomore year, but if you ever saw my school yearbook picture and my homecoming court photos, you can see the change in me. Yes, I was chosen to represent ROTC for the homecoming court. The only thing I can say is, "But God."

CHAPTER 5

It's Time To Leave Familiar

WHILE IN HIGH SCHOOL, I was a member of the Air Force Junior ROTC. I already knew people who had joined the military before going to high school, and they thought it was a good idea that they joined the military. Listening to some of my classmates talk about the class and how it prepares you for the military sounded intriguing so I decided to join. I ended up talking with my guidance counselor about changing my schedule so that I could join. It was one of the best class changes that I asked for during my high school years. I loved being a part of the ROTC; it kept me motivated and wanting more out of life and outside of Florida.

I don't know what it was about the movie "A Few Good Men," but it motivated me even more about my decision to join ROTC, and it hyped me up about joining the military. During my senior year, I was trying to decide what I wanted to do after high school. I was already working at Finish Line in the mall, and it was an excellent job, but I knew I wanted to get out of Florida. So, when the Marine recruiter came to visit the ROTC class, he had me motivated to join the Marines. Now that I think about it, it was the movie "A Few Good Men" and the union that motivated my decision to join the Marines. "Hey, what can I say? We all have our moments." After a while, the recruiter started working my nerves, and I no longer wanted to join the Marines. So from there, I decided to give the Air Force a try since I had a decent Armed Service Vocation Aptitude Battery (ASVAB) test score.

So, I headed to the Air Force recruiter's office, and I remember so distinctly SGT Robertson saying, "You will be by." He was one of the recruiters assigned to the high school for recruiting, and he was Army also. It was as if he knew

I was shopping around, trying to decide which branch of service I would join. All the while, knowing I was going to the Army. God honestly had a plan for my life. I went to the Air Force recruiter's office, and he talked about the different jobs and some of the requirements for joining. I got the information I needed, but before I left, I had to weigh in since the branches had a weight requirement to join. Let me tell you, I was determined with a capital "D." I needed to lose 10 pounds or so, and I went for the cabbage soup diet. All I knew was that I wanted to join the military and get out of the state of Florida and start new.

Just like anything you try, either you keep going or realize that there must be a better way. That's precisely what happened to my Air Force dreams. They flew out the window. I got frustrated with trying to lose weight to the point I was making myself sick. I then went to the Navy recruiter, who again gave me the information I needed to decide whether I wanted to join, and I was pumped. However, during the conversation, he mentioned something about having complete "sea time." Of course, I gave a look, and I thought, "I don't do water, and that's not even going to happen." So, what did I do next? You got it, I walked my way down to the Army recruiter's office and that's all she wrote.

My mind was entirely made up and ready to sign, but the recruiters still needed to come home and talk with papa and grandma. SGT Robertson and the other recruiter came to the house and spoke about the benefits of joining and expectations. Both papa and grandma said it was my decision, and they supported me either way. I was so happy about that indeed. That meant so much to me that they supported my decision to join. I was scared about leaving, but I knew I wanted more for myself, and the only way that would happen was by joining the military.

Now it's time to prepare for graduation and give out my tickets to family members. After talking with papa and grandma about his ticket, I decided to give his ticket to my biological mom so that she could come and see me graduate. Papa wasn't able to attend, so I was able to provide her with his ticket. Plus, I knew he would be there with me in spirit, and I would see him after graduation to show him my diploma. I called my mom and let her know I had a ticket for her, but she would have to find transportation from Tallahassee to Panama City. She was happy, of course, and said that she would work out the transportation with someone in Tallahassee.

It's the day of graduation, and I am so excited to be walking across the stage, getting my diploma and preparing for something new after high school. I was thrilled to see that my mom was able to make it to my graduation, but I wasn't at all happy when I saw who drove her down. When I saw that it was my brother, I was upset deep inside. I said to myself, "This is my day, and he shouldn't be here." I knew I had to get it and keep it together because I was preparing to walk the stage this day. After the graduation was complete and everyone had gone back to the house, I avoided my brother like the plague. I acted as if he didn't even exist. I was trying to forget about the fact that he molested me, and a part of me knew he could sense I wasn't trying to be around him at all. When it was time for him and my mom to head back to Tallahassee, I gave a half-wave and knew it was time to leave

Florida. I knew I had made the right decision to join the military.

CHAPTER 6

The Day My Life Changed: 22 August 1997

FTER I HAD COMPLETED basic training at Fort Jackson, SC, and Advance Individual Training (AIT) at Fort Lee, VA, I received my notification of where my first duty station would be located. I was excited to hear where I would be going, but when I heard I was getting stationed at Schofield Barracks, HI, I wasn't happy anymore. I mean, most people are excited about going to Hawaii, but I am not a water person, and I was fearful of flying. Some of the trainees went back home to do hometown recruiting, which is normal, but I decided to head straight to Hawaii. There are days that I sit back and reflect and know that I should have gone back home, but I didn't.

Already upset and unhappy about getting stationed, I know you are probably thinking as you are reading this, "Who wouldn't be happy to live in Hawaii?" I mean Hawaii of all places. When you are going into the military, there is no telling where you could be stationed. I just know Hawaii wasn't that place for me. At the end of the day, you have to adapt and adjust to your new living environment. My first year in Hawaii came with both ups and downs with trying to fit in and getting adjusted to a new place and people.

One of the good things about being stationed in Hawaii was the organizational days and the different places and venues that units decided to hold them at each year. The first organizational day I attended was held at the Hale Koa Hotel Resort on Waikiki Beach. Before this day, I had called home to check on papa and grandma to make sure they were doing alright and if they needed anything. I had called home a week earlier and asked papa how he was feeling, and he said he wasn't feeling so well. I told him that I hope he feels better and that I was going to be sending some money home to him and grandma. That was the last time I talked to him on the phone. I didn't call that much before his passing. I was still adjusting to military life and living on my own. Not to make any excuses, I know I could have done better by calling home more often than I was.

It's the 22nd of August 1997, and my unit was downtown in Waikiki, enjoying the organizational day activities. During this day, we had a lot going on with both individual and group activities. I was in the water with soldiers from my unit, laughing, talking, and just enjoying the day before we headed back to Schofield. Even during all the enjoyment with my unit, I started feeling so empty inside as if I was losing something. I began to feel sad and didn't know why I was feeling this way until I got back to the barracks and checked my phone for messages. When I checked my messages, I was completely numb and didn't know how to respond.

Checking my voicemail, I heard my cousin Jamesina say, "Call home as soon as possible. Papa passed away." It was like time had frozen. I was in complete disbelief and all I remember was trying to recall the number I needed to call back home on. When I called, she answered the phone, and I asked her what had happened? Papa had passed away from a brain aneurysm. After that, I walked downstairs as calmly as I could. I sat down on the stairs and said, "My papa died." I don't know who came to console me, but I know I was broken. The one thing I remember thinking is he didn't even make it to see his birthday, which was on the 25th and mine's is the 26th.

My Commander, First Sergeant and Supervisor were quick about working to get me home as soon as possible. There was a hold up trying to figure out if I was going to have to pay for my ticket after I received my official Red Cross message. It became an issue because I called him "papa" instead of dad. It got to the point I had to explain I was raised in foster care by him, and I always called him "papa," and it didn't change even after I was adopted. By the grace of God, I had a copy of my birth certificate as well. It

was crazy, but eventually, everything worked itself out, and I was on my way home. That flight
home seemed like it was the longest flight home
in my life. Trying to keep my mind focused, the
one song that kept my mind at ease was God's
Property song, "My Life Is In Your Hands" and
"More Than I Can Bear." If it weren't for those
two songs, I would have lost it on that flight.

The one picture that kept on flashing in my
head was I'm not going to see papa when I open
the door, sitting in his recliner anymore when I
walk into the house. I slept in that recliner when
I was at home for the funeral. There was that
part of me that just needed to be close to him,
and that recliner was the nearest object. My papa
meant the world to me. He introduced me to the
Lord with my first Bible, and my name was engraved on it. He taught me how to say the Lord's
Prayer and blessing before we ate at the din-
ner table. When he would bake a cake, I would
be there right beside him. Me, with my greedy
self, would ask him to save me some of the bat-
ter after it was poured into the baking pan. On
days he would make juleps, I would help him put
them in the freezer so they would be ready for

the next day. Those times with him were truly special to me even to this day. Papa was the one who got me involved in politics. His two favorite channels were C-SPAN, CNN, and of course, the local news. Mind you, I would be thinking to myself, "Can we watch something else?" At the end of the day, it all paid off in school, especially with my government class.

I wasn't the easiest child at times, growing up. I had my moments of talking back, saying things like, "I hated living there," all because I wasn't able to do things I saw other people doing around me. One thing is for sure: His love for me never changed. I could always count on my papa. He was the one consistent man who didn't walk out of my life. He always wanted the best for other people around him and me as well. He honestly had a profound impact on the lives of the children who came into their home, needing to be fostered in their home. Isaiah means "God is my salvation," and he was brought into this world to impact the lives of so many children and to be a blessing to their lives.

CHAPTER 7

The Grip of Depression

FOLLOWING THE DEATH OF papa, I didn't know what I was going to do. There was a part of me that was angry with God that my papa was no longer here. He no longer would be able to call and celebrate his birthday on the 25th of August. His birthday was the day before mine, so the 25th and the 26th of August were always special days to me.

I was depressed to the point that I didn't want to celebrate my birthday, and the month of August was challenging for me to get through. I tried to close the door on the world. Even during my pregnancy, I was depressed to the point

I was surprised that he came into the world a happy baby. I wanted to honor papa by giving my son Johnathan his name. I named him Johnathan Isaiah. I knew that had papa lived, they would have had a great relationship, and Johnathan would have learned a lot from him as well. I struggled as a single parent when Johnathan was first born. I had a great support system around me, which was a blessing, but there was still a part of me that was unhappy.

I was struggling in my finances and still trying to do my best to make sure that Johnathan had everything he needed and wanted for nothing. At that time, I didn't have a car, so I had to depend on others to get me to work and other places that I needed to go. I felt like such a burden on people. Even though they may have necessarily said I wasn't, it was how I was feeling deep inside. I wasn't in the right state of mind. There were times when my bank account was in the negative, and I would have to ask my friends to help me with my finances so I could pay for daycare. I had moments when I felt that Johnathan would have been better off if he had another mom to give him a better life.

During this time, I was barely going to church. This is so sad to say, but I can count on one hand how many times I went to church when I was stationed in Hawaii. At this point in my life, I can honestly say I wasn't trying to do church in any way, shape, form, or fashion. There was that part of me that knew I was sinking and drowning, and pride just kept me at a standstill. As awesome as God is, He is always in control, even when you're out of control. By this time, I was looking for a new babysitter and I got a list of Family Child Care (FCC) who operated out of their homes. When I got the list, God pointed me to one number, and it was the right number. When Rodney and Veronica Brown came into my and Johnathan's life, I knew it was nothing but the hand of the Lord on this divine connection. God was on the scene in a strong and mighty way.

Just being around them gave me so much hope that I was going to make it. Not only in life but in the military as well, regardless if I was a single parent and everything was going to be alright. I knew I had to put in the work to move forward. At that point, getting out of the Army wasn't an option anymore. There was a time I honestly wanted out of the Army in such a bad way, but what would that have accomplished? It would have accomplished nothing but more struggles and mountains to climb. Oftentimes God will remove you from a place of familiarity to get your attention and put you in the place that He has purposed for your life. I had to look beyond what was going on in my life at that time and see the bigger picture that was before me.

I was still dealing with the spirit of fear and doubt, but I had to keep pushing forward. When I met Ms. Annice Jones, Veronica's mother, she was exactly the light I needed in my life at that point and beyond. She fell in love with Johnathan, and he became a part of her heart and family. Now she wasn't going to let me feel sorry for myself. She told me like it was, and it was indeed what I needed in my life. Her encouragement was a reminder that I couldn't give up, and I had to stay the course. Life wasn't over, but I had to learn how to live.

CHAPTER 8

A Change Is Going To Come

After the Browns left Hawaii for their next assignment, I had to start looking for a new babysitter, and God opened another door. October 1998, I was on my way to Fort Stewart, GA, and by the grace of God, I ended up being assigned to Savannah, GA. This was indeed a turning point in my life that God was speaking to my heart. So too was the enemy speaking to my flesh, and I ended up getting involved with people I knew I shouldn't have allowed myself to get attached. I was simply a lonely girl looking for love and attention. I was losing myself all over again, sinking back deeper into depression. I was still struggling to be a good mom and a good soldier.

I found myself back in a place, asking God why He allowed me to be Johnathan's mom. I was struggling with myself because I honestly felt like I was doing a horrible job as a mom. I thought I wasn't giving him enough as a mom, but somehow I knew it was nothing but the grace of God I was able to provide for him. One thing I always purposed was that Johnathan would have been better even if I had to go without.

Georgia was my time and place to reconnect with God, as well as Veronica, Rodney and Ms. Jones. I would go to Atlanta on my four-day weekends, and it was a blessed time. Rodney, Veronica, and Ms. Jones were always ministering to me the Word of God and His faithfulness to those who trust and believe in Him no matter the situation. I grew up in church, so I knew God's Word was true, and it never changes. With everything that was going on in my life, I had stepped away from the Lord. I can honestly say it seemed like it was a struggle to get back to the Lord. Even in my seek, God had a plan for me to return to what I knew was true—His Word and faithfulness. When there is a call and purpose on your life, He won't let you go. I am a living witness to that in my life.

One unforgettable trip that I made to Atlanta is when God spoke into my life during a Bible study. I went to a Wednesday night Bible study with Ms. Jones and the Word was going forth so mighty, and the anointing was heavy on Pastor Betty. As she was prophesying over people, there was a part of me saying to myself, "Please God don't have her come over here." I am barely living right, and I don't want the Lord telling all my business when I already know I'm not living right. Well, of course, the Lord wasn't listening to me, and she began prophesying into my life. She told me the Lord was going to use me to evangelize into the lives of young women, and I was an evangelist.

In my small mind, I'm already crying, thinking, why would God want to use someone like me to speak into the lives of anyone? There is nothing right about my life right now. I was so living out of His will. Who was I that God would want to use me? She asked me if I received it, and I said, "Yes ma'am," but deep in my heart, I kept saying, "Lord, I'm not fit to serve You."

My life wasn't going right at the time, even though I had received this Word from the Lord. I was involved with people I had no business with all. I was still struggling with my finances. I'm drowning in sin. All I saw was a horrible person when I looked at myself in the mirror. There was one particular night I was lying on the couch trying to get some sleep and my mind was racing all over the place. When I looked in the kitchen, I saw this black figure standing there waving at me as if it was saying, "We are here." I was terrified because, again, I wasn't living right and so outside of the will of God. I took it as a sign that I had no choice but to get myself together, get right and real with the Lord, and stop playing around.

It was time for me to choose my next assignment, and all that was on my mind was Alaska. I had Alaska on my brain so bad that it's the only place I could think of. When my reenlistment Noncommissioned Officer (NCO) said, it was available, I was so elated. However, I allowed a misguided decision to change my mind about going to Alaska to go to Germany. That was a dumb move on my part, but God was working behind the scenes, even with my decision and changing my mind. Little did I know that God was using this decision to put me back in a right relationship with Him. I was trying to get to Germany for a person, but God was sending me there for my purpose.

Before I left for Germany, my prayer to God was asking Him to put people in my life that He purposed to be in my life. I realized that I was making the wrong decision about the people I allowed in my life—some for the good and some for the bad. I just knew I wanted different, and I needed better for not only me, but for Johnathan. Even before I left for Germany, I had a dream about the ministry I would be attending before I got to Germany. I started back attending church and was happy to be back in the fold. This completely opened my heart and mind to know that God heard my prayers. Not only for myself, but for Johnathan as well. The backslider came back home, and I had no intention of going back to work. Did I make mistakes along the way? Yes, I did, but God kept His hand upon my life.

CHAPTER 9

The Time Has Come

GERMANY IS THE PLACE where I honestly had a turning point hearing the voice of the Lord. When I got to Germany, I was by myself getting settled in before I went back stateside to get Johnathan. My biggest obstacle at that point was getting my European driver's license so that I could get my vehicle out of storage. Anyone who has been to Europe will tell you that the test is interesting. I ended up having to take that test four times. I was studying like I was studying for a midterm to get to the next semester. One Sunday, we had a guest speaker at the church I was attending, and the word she brought forth was powerful. The guest speaker was Mother Johnson.

Mother Johnson is a real powerhouse in the Lord, and when she spoke, you knew you were hearing from the Lord indeed. This particular Sunday that she was visiting was the day before I was supposed to take my driver's test for the fourth time. She ministered to the whole body, and to individuals as the Holy Spirit was leading her throughout the service. While she was going around, she stopped at me, put her hand on my head and spoke, "You've studied, and the Lord said you have already passed the test." I have been prophesied to before, but that prophetic word fell into place like a puzzle piece that was missing. During that time, I was working on getting Johnathan into school before I went back stateside to bring him over to Germany. At this point, they had opened head-start for students, and the one disqualifier for me was a Sergeant, and the program was more for a Specialist and below. It was in my heart to apply and I did, and Johnathan was accepted; two wins in a week. I passed the driving test that week, which I know my supervisor was happy because he didn't have to pick me up for work anymore. I was on my way home to pack-up Johnathan and finally bring him to Germany.

Having been in head start growing up, I was excited that he was going to be able to take part in it rather than waiting a whole year for school. Although I was very excited about having Johnathan in Head Start, I would soon face a horrible accusation that I was abusing my own son. This particular day I had dropped off Johnathan on my way to staff duty. While in class, he was messing with a poster on the wall, and I gently tapped his hand and said, "Don't pull that down." If I thought a tap on the hand would have me talking with health care officials and someone from the Criminal Investigation Division (CID), I would have thought twice.

I was getting off from duty, and I went by the office to talk with my supervisor before I left to get Johnathan. She just looked me in the face and said you can't see Johnathan. Of course, I'm trying to figure out why in the world I can't see my son. That's when she told me that his teacher reported that I was abusive to him and needless to say, I was mad, angry, devastated, and upset. I was imagining him being in foster care. I was thinking in my heart, I can't lose custody of my son. I would never in my life put him in a situation to have anyone thinking I was abusing him. I was in the system, and I know how that is. The investigator spoke with people who knew me personally and interacted with myself and Johnathan. I was honest with them and told them exactly what had transpired in the classroom. There was no need to make something appear that wasn't. After all of that was closed, Johnathan was removed from that teacher's classroom.

Germany was my new foundation to reestablish my relationship with God. Johnathan was with me, and that was a blessing within itself. As I am writing this paragraph, I can hear him say, "Mommy come here." I would go upstairs walking into his room, and his reply was, "Mommy, I love you." Often, he would yell from his room at any random moment, "Mommy, I love you." He loved his PlayStation so he would ask me to come and watch him play a game. Never a dull moment. I had been a single mother my entire military career and having Johnathan with me throughout my career was indeed a blessing.

In 2005, I was preparing to go on my first deployment in support of Operation Iraqi Freedom. I had to make preparations for Johnathan while I would be away for a year. So much was going on at that time because I was also being assigned to a new unit and getting settled into a new section. Before I was set to depart, and I had everything taken care of for Johnathan while I was away, I had lunch with Apostle Archie and one of my sisters in Christ. During the lunch, he asked me if I was ready for the deployment, and in that same sentence, he said you know this is when you are going to bring your first word. Me being me, I was looking at him like "okay." This was the time for me to truly get ready for what was going to take place during this deployment, but I was second-guessing myself yet again. I rejected my own self and how God said He would use me. I saw myself small in God's eyes, but of course, He sees our beginning and end.

Just as God said it was going to be, I brought my first message, and I was wholly involved in the gospel services during the deployment from the praise and worship and dance ministry. Praise dancing would not only bring me closer to Christ, but it's the one place in the world, I honestly felt completely close to Him. I love the dance ministry. It's a place of peace and talking with the Lord through the movement of dance. I learned so much from the leader over the dance ministry from being a dance leader from the purpose of colors, fasting, scriptures, choreography, and the purpose of and flow of ministry.

One Wednesday Bible study, the topic was on forgiveness and unforgiveness. The lesson was powerful and on time. I was taking notes like crazy. Little did I know that this very lesson was preparing me to deal with a personnel issue I wasn't ready for. The next day while I was at work, I received a Red Cross message that I needed to go home and take care of a loved one. I was not ready for this at all. The deployment was going well. I was on fire for the Lord, and deeply involved in the gospel service, but I had to go home and take care of a family issue. Often, we never know why some things happen, but God has a way of preparing us too. We won't be surprised or caught off guard.

Once I got back from emergency leave, we had four months left to go, and I was making plans on some of the changes I needed to make once I got back to Germany. Arriving back in July, I visited the church my brother in Christ was attending after coming back from deployment. The atmosphere in the house was filled with God's presence. I knew this was the place He wanted me in. I prayed and asked God what I needed to do regarding changing ministries, and He gave me the peace I needed to move on from that ministry.

Once I got settled entirely back in Germany, I went back stateside to bring Johnathan with me, and he was a handful because we had been apart for so long and needed to reconnect. Now that I had started attending the new ministry, I had become very active in the church, working with the youth and teen ministry, as well as the dance ministry. There was something about the praise dance ministry, where I always felt so connected to the Lord. I could hear a song, and the moves would download, and I could express how I was feeling.

During my time at the ministry, I connected with the Camarillo family and they too, were a God sent for myself and Johnathan. Pastor Shawn Camarillo was that one person who connected to Johnathan like a magnet. He could be acting up in church, and she would call him over and he would get himself together. He was a busybody and yes, the candy did work, but I know all she had to do was talk with him and Johnathan would be good. Little did I know that the Camarillo family, Pastors Jesse and Shawn would become a truly vital part of our lives even after we all departed from Germany at different times.

CHAPTER 10

I Almost Let Go

GOD MAY NOT BE listening in the way we expect Him to be listening, but trust me, He is, and He will show up in a way you know it's Him. It seemed like life had me pinned up against a brick wall. You may be thinking how a believer can be so dissatisfied with their life? If they say they believe God and know He is real, then what is the problem? Speaking for myself, I was still in a place in my life where I honestly hadn't allowed myself to be loved by anyone, especially God. I would reflect on losing people and things in my life and I would question what in the world was wrong with me? I hadn't healed from the passing of papa, and that would still follow me until I allowed God to heal my heart.

I had fallen back into a place where I was self-loathing all over again. I felt as if I could be a better parent, person, soldier, friend, etc. In my mind, the enemy had a running scene by scene movement, and every clip was from a negative place in my life. The enemy was planting a seed of doubt and I was getting frustrated and sad and all I wanted to do was be by myself. I started back questioning my purpose on earth and why I was still even here.

In 2008, probably about a year after coming back from the deployment, I went to the Real Women's Conference with some of the ladies at church. I can't remember the theme for that year, but this conference was right on time for me, and it was a breakthrough that I needed in my life. The conference was on fire and the Spirit of the Lord was heavy and the atmosphere of deliverance was indeed in the place. The "come to Jesus" moment for me was during the play that was presented. In part of the play, one of the females was indeed at her breaking point in life. She was on the brink of giving up. It was a place I could relate. The praise dancer came out and the song "I Almost Let Go," started playing and even before the second verse of the song, I broke. That song spoke to every emotion and how I was feeling at the time and where I was in my life — both mentally and spiritually.

I was at the point where I wanted to give up and completely throw in the towel. While listening to a song and truly hearing the words, I knew God heard my prayers and words of confession and affirmations during the conference. I started blessing God that He heard me, and He wasn't about to let me take my life, and depression wasn't my portion for my life. Through everything that I had been through, God was showing me I had a purpose and I wasn't here to be like other people. I am here to be who He called me to be. After the conference, I held onto Psalms 139:13-14 (KJV), For thou hast possessed my reins: thou hast covered me in my mother's womb. I will praise thee; for I am fearfully and wonderfully made: marvelous are thy works; and that my soul knoweth right well. This scripture kept me grounded and helped me trust God in the midst of what my natural eyes perceived.

CHAPTER 11

The Father Never Leaves Us

*T*HROUGHOUT MY LIFE, BAT-
TLING with depression, rejection,
and thoughts of suicide, one area of
my life that was always a constant was God. He
always kept positive and faithful men and wom-
en of God in my life. No matter where I went,
God had people speaking into my life. There
were and are those who wouldn't allow me to
have a pity party. Yes, there were times I would
think to myself. "I don't have time to hear this."
Did I feel like their words of rebuke and correction could have come a little softer? Yes, but me
being the person I am, God knows how to get

my attention? Did I ever once think like I'm not coming around them anymore? I could have, but that wasn't going to happen. I didn't need people around me to sugar coat. I needed realness and truth.

As you read this, you are probably like "child, I would have gotten up and walked away." Looking at it like that, that's the easy way out. That is also the way the enemy desires to pull us from the people God has purposed and ordained to be in our lives. For myself, God used people He knew would be firm, hold me accountable for my actions, and stay on the path He purposed for me. I was allowing the world and the enemy to have power over me, and I could get upset because I was letting it happen. One thing I had to learn, and I hold on to this saying, "power given is power taken." The only time someone or something can have power over you is if you willfully give it over. I was reminded that God hadn't forgotten about me and to stay in the press. Stay in the fight. Hands down, I had to stop "helping" the Lord and let Him work. I will admit I thought I could get over my depression

by myself, but even mighty men and women of
God in the Bible still needed help from the Lord.

By this time, I had moved to Killeen, Texas
(Fort Hood), and the Lord guided my footsteps
to an excellent ministry that I was continuing to
grow in. I was working with the children's ministry, praise dance and on the ministerial staff.
God was doing some great work in my life, and I
am so grateful. Out of nowhere, the Camarillo's
moved to Texas and just that like we were back
in each other's lives, and it was an appointed
time. I could and still to this day, be transparent
and talk with them about anything going on in
my life. Their wisdom and guidance are always
invaluable.

God will take you from a place of familiar and
put you in a place where He needs you to grow
in every aspect of your life. When I moved to
Killeen, Texas, I knew that God was establish-
ing me to move forward, not only in purpose but
in growth. From strengthening me in my prayer
life and fasting, God is opening doors for me to
walk in my calling and purpose. This was my
time for believing and not doubting even with

the mistakes I made while God was making me into the woman of God that He purposed me to be. Often, we need to move in order for us to grow. If we continue to stay in a place that makes us comfortable, why should we expect to grow? If the Holy Spirit is your compass, you will never get off course.

CHAPTER 12

Everlasting Love: Jeremiah 31:3

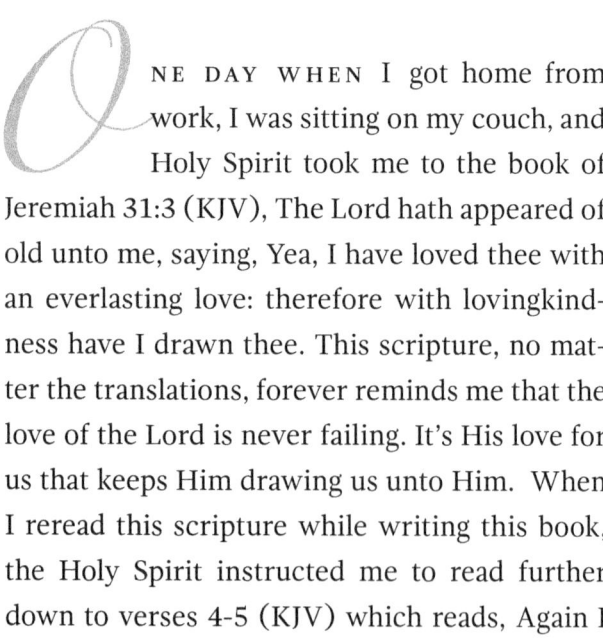

ONE DAY WHEN I got home from work, I was sitting on my couch, and Holy Spirit took me to the book of Jeremiah 31:3 (KJV), The Lord hath appeared of old unto me, saying, Yea, I have loved thee with an everlasting love: therefore with lovingkindness have I drawn thee. This scripture, no matter the translations, forever reminds me that the love of the Lord is never failing. It's His love for us that keeps Him drawing us unto Him. When I reread this scripture while writing this book, the Holy Spirit instructed me to read further down to verses 4-5 (KJV) which reads, Again I will build thee, and thou shalt be built, O virgin of Israel: thou shalt again be adorned with thy tabrets, and shalt go forth in the dances of them that make merry. Thou shalt yet plant vines upon the mountains of Samaria: the planters shall plant, and shall eat them as common things.

God always had an undying love for the children of Israel. Even in their disobedience, He yet still had love for them. The love of the Lord never changes and is constant and consistent even when we aren't. God was always sending out His prophets to remind them to get back in line with the will of God and His purpose for His people. Just as the Lord was telling the children of Israel, I created you to be in relationship and fellowship with me, not with the world. I so desperately want to have a relationship with you. My heart longs for you to be in My presence.

Although Jeremiah was known as the weeping prophet who went before the Lord on behalf of the children of Israel, we too have had and continue to have our grandmother, grandfathers, mothers, fathers, etc., who have gone before the Lord on our behalf as well so that we can see the value the Lord places on our lives. We have to stop giving the enemy power over us and allowing our view to be blocked by his lies and deception. There is more and God desires to give you more. Power given is power taken and the more we provide Him with the access, He has the victory over our lives.

God wants you to know today that you have value, and your value rests in Him. He validated you the day he placed you in your mother's womb. Even before your father and mother came together, God approved your life and stamped purpose on you. He already knows that you will have bumps in the road, and you will make mistakes, but He will never leave nor forsake you. Nothing in God is by happenstance. God is a good and loving Father who wants what's best for His children. His love is true and faithful and will not run out. Your life has value because you are created in the image and likeness of God.

Although you may have allowed the enemy to have reign in your life, God is saying to you, "My hand is upon your life, and I am waiting on you to come home. I love you with an ever-lasting love that will never fail or change. The enemy has to go. My grace is sufficient for you, for His strength is made perfect in weakness. I come so that you may have life and a life more abundantly."

Prayer of Strength and Restoration

FATHER, I LIFT UP the reader of this book to you. I speak Your peace over their lives and their minds. I come against every negative thought and work of the enemy that has come against their lives, from the standard of the world: family curses, word curses, generational curses, and the words they have spoken against themselves. Father, they are free to be used by You for your glory and your will. Let them recognize who they are in You and You have marked them for purpose and greatness. I uproot the spirit of depression and rejection. They no longer have power over them. The very ground that the seed was planted has been destroyed by the Power of the Blood, in the Name of Jesus. I decree and declare life, freedom and restoration over them, in the mighty name of Jesus. I thank You, Lord for every prodigal son and daughter who are returning to You in this season for divine healing and restoration. Lord, thank You for receiving them back with Your arms wide open. Their minds are renewed and set free in You. This is a day of freedom. They are fearfully and wonderfully made, and the thoughts that You have towards them are good and not of evil. You plan to prosper them with a hope and future. Your love towards them is consistent and never failing. I thank You for the angels that you have assigned to them, and that the Holy Spirit is their GPS to continue to lead and guide them into all truths according to your Word. Keep them covered under the shadow of Your mighty hands. I thank You for the blood that covers their lives, their families, and generations to come in Jesus's mighty precious and wonderful name, I pray. Amen.

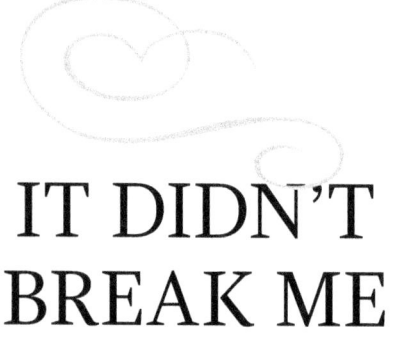

IT DIDN'T BREAK ME

"DEPRESSION"

Though the storms came, Waves constantly
roared

The Warrior in me found determination to
LOUDLY say,

Here I stand BATTERED, BRUISED with tears
flowing down my face

You thought you BROKE me

But it pushed me to my DESTINY

God has given me purpose

I stand STRONGER by the Grace of God

IT DIDN'T BREAK ME

His hand IS on my life, He WON'T allow me to fail

Every trial that I faced; it was the Hand of God PUSHING me

To MY DESTINY

#itdidntbreakme

By

Jennifer Jackson

About The Author

JENNIFER M. JACKSON IS originally from Panama City, Florida. From the time she was five years old, she was involved in ministry. She was singing in her local church's Start Light Choir, a member of the Ushers Youth Department, Youth Secretary, and a member of the Youth Choir. She dedicated her life to Christ at the age of 12 and has been serving ever since. She currently serves in the United States Army with over 25 years of military service. Joining straight out of high school, her military travels have opened the door for her to serve in different ministries cultivating her love for Christ. During these assignments, she worked with both the Children and

Teen Ministries. She was serving as both a ministry head and teacher. During serving in these ministries, she realized her passion for working with the youth and inspiring them to be all they can be in Christ. She is also a praise dancer. She serves at Kingdom First Worship Center in Killen, TX, under the leadership of Pastors Warren and Linda Thames.

She serves as a Logistic NCO in the United States Army. Throughout her time in the military, her assignments have taken her to Hawaii, Hunter Army Airfield, GA, Kaiserslautern, Germany, Israel, Tbilisi, Georgia (the country), Italy, Fort Hood, TX, Fort Bliss, TX, and to her present assignment in Fort Polk, LA. During her military service, she has deployed to Iraq in support of Operation Iraqi Freedom (OEF) and Afghanistan in support of both Operation Enduring Freedom (OEF) and Operation Resolute Support (ORS). She knows that God has placed her there to grow and empower others with each assignment she has been on. She strives to inspire others to not only grow in their walk with Christ but to look beyond their present state and know that the best is yet to come in their lives. She is a credentialed Department of Defense Sexual Assault Response Coordinator (SARC) and Credentialed Advocate (CA). She received a National Organization for Victims Assistance (NOVA) Honorary Award for her tireless efforts to advance crime victims' rights. She is a court-appointed Court Appointed Special Advocate (CASA) / Guardian ad Litem (GAL) for Louisiana.

She has a bachelor's degree in Early Childhood Education from Liberty University. She has one son named Johnathan, who has followed her throughout her military career. She is a collector of dolphins because of their natural smile and innate nature to be a helper. She loves bowling, writing, reading, decorating, and her favorite pastime is football (Tampa Buccaneers and Florida State Seminoles).

Contact Information:
Jennifer M Jackson
chosen@kalledoutandsetapart.me

Index

H

support system, 44

T

Tallahassee, 16, 17, 22, 24, 35
teacher, 23, 28, 29, 55, 56, 77
tears, 24, 74
Teen Ministries, 77
television, 8
Texas, 66
ticket, 34, 35, 40
toddler, 12
torment, 3
towel, 3, 4, 11, 63
trial, 75
trouble, 10, 11, 21, 22, 25
trust, 48, 61, 63
truth, 24, 65

U

unforgiveness, 22, 58
unhappy, 38, 44
upset, 35, 38, 55, 65
usher board, 19

Y